A Study Guide
Hello, Daddy

Richard A. Honeycutt

with
Betty Jane Honeycutt

Parson's Porch

Parson's Porch Books

To order additional copies of this book, contact:

Parson's Porch & Company
1-423-475-7308
www.parsonsporchbooks.com

Introduction

Hello, Daddy was written to help Christians grow in their prayer life. This workbook offers a systematic approach to enhance that growth. It can be used as a study guide for individuals, for formal sessions, or for informal small group work. Used in conjunction with the complete text of *Hello, Daddy*, it will stimulate the reader's thinking so as to give the "still, small voice" maximum opportunity to lead. Although *Hello, Daddy* contains many Scripture passages, we suggest that the reader keep one or more favorite translations of the Bible at hand for reference during study.

Rather than adopt the common elementary-school approach to designing a workbook, we have applied our decades of experience in teaching adults, heavily influenced by two models: Jesus of Nazareth and Socrates of Athens. From Jesus, we come to appreciate teaching by examples from daily life; and we learn that truth, like the Kingdom of God, is encountered within. From Socrates we discern the value of carefully chosen questions in helping the learner to discover truth for him/herself, a method that proves far more effective than authoritarian lecturing or the "find the answer and fill in the blank" methods.

Most of the chapters in this guide are designed to be read before the corresponding chapter in the full text of *Hello, Daddy*. Thus they will help steer your focus when you read the full chapter.

As our readers certainly know, the rewards of a vital prayer life are beyond reckoning. We hope our efforts will assist in achieving this goal.

What Is Prayer?

A. Before reading the chapter "What is Prayer?" in *Hello, Daddy*, give some thought to what our society means by the word "prayer". If you wish, jot down a few brief definitions.

_____

_____

_____

_____

_____

_____

B. List the first few purposes of prayer that you think come to mind for most people (yourself included) when prayer is mentioned.

_____

_____

_____

_____

_____

_____

C. Outline a visit with a friend.

_____

_____

_____

_____

_____

_____

D. Now read the chapter "What is Prayer?" in Hello, Daddy.

E. How much formal preparation do you need before you pray?
    (Careful: first clarify in your mind what you mean by
    "formal".) This answer will vary from person to person; there
    is no universal right or wrong answer.

_____

_____

_____

_____

_____

_____

D. How would you summarize your own aims in praying to God?

_____

_____

_____

_____

_____

_____

How Is Prayer Possible?

A. Before reading the chapter "How Is Prayer Possible?", consider: how would you describe God? Select a few words or phrases that you might use if you met someone who had no concept of God, and you wanted to convey what "God" means.

_____

_____

_____

_____

_____

_____

B. Would your description of God contain any ideas about the relationship between humans and God? If so, what ideas would these be?

_____

_____

_____

_____

_____

_____

C. Would you tend to describe this relationship primarily in terms such as creator, political leader (king), family terms (father-mother), or some other comparison with common experience (co-pilot)?

_____

_____

_____

_____

_____

_____

D. What do you think might be needed for you to communicate with this creator, king, patriarch, matriarch, co-pilot, or whatever term you chose? Would you need special arrangements for conducting a meeting?

_____

_____

_____

_____

_____

_____

E. Read the chapter "How Is Prayer Possible?"

F. Would the special arrangements you considered in question D be related to holiness, in the broad sense in which the word is defined in this chapter?

_____

_____

_____

_____

_____

_____

Beginning in the late nineteenth century, a "Holiness movement" sprang up from John Wesley's "Christian perfection" teaching. This movement has had a profound effect upon evangelical Christianity, and perhaps an even more profound effect upon the secular conception of Christianity. In many cases, the Holiness doctrine has been misrepresented as rule-based religion. While it is not our intent to go into this doctrine or its manifestation in Christian churches in the last century-and-a-half, it is important to recall the true meaning of "holiness" as presented in Chapter 3. The Pharisees of Jesus's time were "Holiness Jews". We can still fall into their errors if we focus too narrowly on the "thou-shalt-not's" rather than the purpose emphasized by Jesus in his teachings.

G. Can you find at least four places in the New Testament where purpose is emphasized as central to the Christian life?

_____

_____

_____

_____

_____

_____

How about in the Old Testament? (Hint: try the Prophets.)

_____

_____

_____

_____

_____

H. When we pray, is it somehow "spiritual" to think and speak of ourselves as "unworthy"? What is true humility, and how do we express it as we relate to God?

_____

_____

_____

_____

_____

I. Who is more holy: a person who consistently badmouths him/herself, or a person who expresses self-acceptance and self-esteem as (s)he helps and serves others?

_____

_____

_____

_____

_____

_____

J. Which comes first: holiness or a relationship with God? (Don't worry, this one doesn't have an answer that receives universal agreement. But thinking about it is a good exercise! James 1:27 contains a valuable hint.)

_____

_____

_____

_____

_____

_____

K. Do Matthew 25:31-46, Ephesians 2:8, and James 1:22 help you to understand how we are to live in attunement with God?

_____

_____

_____

_____

_____

_____

To Whom Do You Pray?

A. Before reading the chapter "To Whom Do You Pray?", can you think of two ways in which God, as revealed by Jesus, differs from an ideal earthly monarch?

_____

_____

_____

_____

_____

_____

B. What is God's Name? Does it matter what we think his Name is?

_____

_____

_____

_____

_____

_____

_____

Father

C. Recall your answers to the first four questions for the chapter "How Is Prayer Possible?" If you specifically focus on your heart rather than your rational mind, would these answers be different? How?

_____

_____

_____

_____

_____

_____

D. How would you describe the ideal father?

_____

_____

_____

_____

_____

_____

E. How did your own biological father compare to this ideal?

_____

_____

_____

_____

_____

_____

Was your own father aware of his limitations? How might his background and circumstances have influenced his parenting?

_____

_____

_____

_____

_____

_____

_____

F. Read the chapter "To Whom Do You Pray?"

G. Can you relate to God as your ideal Father, or has the word "father" become so contaminated for you that you need to find another way to represent God's relationship to you? (Language should be our servant, not our master.) Comment.

_____

_____

_____

_____

_____

_____

H. What parts of our society's concepts of God may have become so contaminated that the word interferes with our relationship with God? For example, does the word "God" have good connotations for everyone? How can we think and talk about God in a way that helps us feel God's love and care, and helps us feel love for God? Are there some common "religious" ideas about God that we should emphasize more? Are there some that we should de-emphasize?

_____

_____

_____

_____

_____

_____

I. What are your own personal feelings about God as Father ... as Mother?

_____

_____

_____

_____

_____

_____

Our Father

J. Consider in family terms: What is your own relationship with God? (Would you say you are God's daughter or son?)

_____

_____

_____

_____

_____

_____

What relationship do you think friends and acquaintances of your own religious tradition have with God? (Would you say they are daughters and sons of God?)

_____

_____

_____

_____

_____

What relationship do you think those who are not of your religious tradition have with God? (Would you say they are children of God, enemies of God, or strangers to God?)

_____

_____

_____

_____

_____

Based on these three answers, what is your relationship with others of your own religion? ... of other religions? (Brothers and sisters, cousins, friends, enemies?)

_____

_____

_____

_____

_____

_____

If you are stuck on the last question, try reading Genesis 1:27 and Hebrews 11:6.

K. Does it feel sacrilegious to call ourselves God's children, and Jesus's sisters and brothers?

_____

_____

_____

_____

_____

_____

L. How do you feel about the idea that God may have held fatherly feelings toward Adolph Hitler and Joseph Stalin? How about a modern politician whom you dislike or distrust? A person who has wronged you? Could you pray "Our Father" with this person?

_____

_____

_____

_____

_____

_____

In the Heavens

M. Is it important to you to think of God as being in a particular physical location? If so, where is that location, and why is it important to think of God being there?

_____

_____

_____

_____

_____

_____

N. If God is in some physical location (as the ancient Jews thought He lived in Jerusalem), does that imply that he is not in other places as well? What does Psalm 139 say about this?

_____

_____

_____

_____

_____

_____

O. Given the line of thought presented in the sidebar at right, what did Jesus mean by specifying Our Father *in the heavens*?

_____

_____

_____

_____

_____

_____

If we were created as spiritual beings—as Dr. William Tiller of Stanford University says, "spiritual beings having a physical experience"—then physical locations must be somehow less real than spiritual realities such as ourselves and God. Difficult as it is for us to accept the idea that space and time do not define ultimate reality, modern physics (at least in the Big Bang Theory) has concluded that space and time began with the Big Bang. What happened before the Big Bang? Wrong question! There was no time, so there could not have been a "before". What is outside the space of our universe? Wrong question again! The universe is defined as including all of space-time, so there is no "outside".

Perhaps another way to think about this is to realize that love which we feel or express can be the most powerful force we experience, but where is love located? We can agree to call the state of God's Being by the name "heaven" or "the heavens", but there is no need to identify that state exclusively with any physical location.

P. How do we balance the "otherness" of God "in the heavens" with the personal nature of "Our Father"? How can overemphasizing either aspect interfere with our fellowship with God?

_____

_____

_____

_____

_____

_____

Hallowed Be Your Name

A. Why would Jesus have suggested that we pray, "hallowed be your name"?

_____

_____

_____

_____

_____

_____

B. In what ways do we properly hallow God's name?

_____

_____

_____

_____

_____

_____

C. In what ways do we abuse God's name?

_____

_____

_____

_____

_____

_____

D. Read Matthew 12:36. How does this passage tie in with our prayer that God's name be hallowed?

_____

_____

_____

_____

_____

_____

E. Read the chapter "Hallowed Be Your Name".

F. Would you say that "Hallowed be your name" is more of a prayer or an affirmation of our relationship with God? Comment.

_____

_____

_____

_____

_____

_____

Thy Kingdom Come, Thy Will Be Done, On Earth As In Heaven

Thy Kingdom, Thy Will

A. Have you seen a translation of the Bible in which some of the text is set out in the form of poetry? How does it affect your understanding of a passage if you think of it as poetry? For example, do you understand the Psalms differently than historical passages from Kings and Chronicles?

_____

_____

_____

_____

_____

_____

B. Have you ever been in an organization in which two or more people became embroiled in a "territorial dispute"? Such disputes are often about who has the power and responsibility over a certain part of the work. The "territory" in these cases is not real-estate. How does it influence your understanding of "the kingdom of Heaven" if you do not think of it as being like a country on Earth?

_____

_____

_____

_____

_____

Thy Will Be Done

C. In your heart of hearts, what do you think is God's will for your life?

_____

_____

_____

_____

_____

_____

Are you enthusiastic about God's will being done in your life?

_____

_____

_____

_____

_____

_____

D. What do you think is God's will for the world and its people?

_____

_____

_____

_____

E. Do you feel comfortable trusting God with your future, knowing that the results may not be as you would have planned?

_____

_____

_____

_____

_____

_____

F. How does God's will interact with our free will?

_____

_____

_____

_____

_____

_____

G. Is everything that happens to us God's will? Explain your answer.

_____

_____

_____

_____

_____

_____

H. How should we respond to troubling events in our lives? (What
   does James 1:2 say? Is this easy to do?)

_____

_____

_____

_____

_____

I. When you are stumped about a choice or situation in your life,
    you need wisdom. What are three ways of receiving wisdom?

_____

_____

_____

_____

_____

On Earth As In Heaven

J. What stands in the way of God's will being done on Earth as in Heaven?

_____

_____

_____

_____

_____

_____

Give Us This Day Our Daily Bread

What Kind of Bread?

A. What does the phrase "daily bread" bring to mind?

_____

_____

_____

_____

_____

_____

B. Do you think it is sacrilegious to think of food for the body rather than "spiritual food" as "daily bread"?

_____

_____

_____

_____

_____

_____

C. Is the series, "spirit, soul, and body" listed in order of
importance? Is one more important than the other?

_____

_____

_____

_____

_____

If the body is the temple of the Holy Spirit (I Cor. 6:19), is it to be
despised or honored?

_____

_____

_____

_____

_____

D. How should we receive our daily bread from our Daddy? With
greed? With a sense of unworthiness? With gratitude? With
intention to put it to use according to our best understanding of
our Daddy's will?

_____

_____

_____

_____

_____

Our Work

E. What aspects of your work do you consider to be gifts from God?

_____

_____

_____

_____

_____

_____

F. Are there challenging aspects of your work in which you need God's help for direction and understanding?

_____

_____

_____

_____

_____

_____

Our Dependence Upon God

G. What is the source of your supply for physical needs? Your job? Must we "work for a living"? What does Luke 12:32 mean?

_____

_____

_____

_____

_____

_____

H. Is there any such thing as a "self-made man" (or woman)? Why or why not?

_____

_____

_____

_____

_____

_____

Spiritual Food

I. What is "spiritual food"? (No one-word answers, please!)

_____

_____

_____

_____

_____

_____

J. What did Jesus mean when he said he is the bread that came
    down from Heaven?

_____

_____

_____

_____

_____

_____

K. In what ways do we receive "spiritual food"?

_____

_____

_____

_____

_____

_____

And Forgive Us our Offenses, as We Forgive Our Offenders

A. Why do you think Jesus tied forgiveness on our part with being given our daily bread?

_____

_____

_____

_____

_____

Offenses

A. What do these words mean to you:

Debts

_____

Sins

_____

Trespasses

_____

Offenses

_____

B. Are all sins committed against God? Explain your answer.

_____

_____

_____

_____

_____

_____

C. When we sin against another human, can we always make up
    for it? Sometimes?

_____

_____

_____

_____

_____

_____

D. When we sin against God, can we ever make up for it? Do we
    need to?

_____

_____

_____

_____

_____

Being Forgiven

C. What does God's forgiveness do for us? (This requires more than a one-point answer.)

_____

_____

_____

_____

_____

_____

D. Are we supposed to feel guilty after we sin? Why or why not?

_____

_____

_____

_____

_____

_____

E. What are we supposed to do after we sin?

_____

_____

_____

_____

_____

_____

Forgiving Others

I. Why is it so hard to forgive others?

_____

_____

_____

_____

_____

_____

J. Do we have to **feel** that we've forgiven the person who offended against us? How, exactly, do we forgive?

_____

_____

_____

_____

_____

_____

Forgiving Ourselves

K. Why is it so hard to forgive ourselves?

_____

_____

_____

_____

_____

_____

L. Why is it so important to forgive ourselves?

_____

_____

_____

_____

_____

_____

M. What is the unforgivable sin?

_____

_____

_____

_____

_ _

And Lead Us To Avoid Temptation;
Save Us From the Evil

A. Where does evil come from?

_____

_____

_____

_____

_____

_____

B. Where does temptation come from?

_____

_____

_____

_____

_____

_____

C. Is "deliver us from evil" a prayer for God to rule our every decision, or a prayer of protection? What difference does it make which kind of prayer this is?

_____

_____

_____

_____

_____

_____

D. Can we blame evil and temptations on the Devil? If not, does that imply that there is no Devil? Is the Devil's behavior our responsibility? Just what is our responsibility?

_____

_____

_____

_____

_____

_____

Other Forms of Prayer

A. Aside from the model prayer, how many forms of prayer can you think of without looking at the subheads below? List them.

_____

_____

_____

_____

_____

_____

B. Has the issue of formality—thinking you needed to know just what to say and how to say it—ever gotten in the way of your prayer life? If so, what did you do about that?

_____

_____

_____

_____

_____

_____

Prayer of Thanksgiving

C. Do you find it easy to be thankful for good things in your life? How about for things that do not seem good, or are perhaps really bad?

_____

_____

_____

_____

_____

D. In a single word, what do we need in order to be thankful in circumstances that seem bad to us?

_____

E. Can you think of several reasons that it is important for us to express thankfulness?

_____

_____

_____

_____

_____

_____

Praise

F. Why do we praise God?

_____

_____

_____

_____

_____

_____

Petition

G. What do we seek to change when we petition God: God's mind, circumstances, other people, ourselves?

_____

_____

_____

_____

_____

_____

H. When do we need to say "thy will be done"? With each prayer, or with our whole lives?

_____

_____

_____

_____

_____

_____

I. How do prayers of petition work?

_____

_____

_____

_____

_____

_____

Prayer of Intercession

J. Why pray for others, when God loves them even more than we do?

_____

_____

_____

_____

_____

_____

Ritual Prayer

K. What is the purpose of ritual prayer? Is ritual prayer important? Is it important for everyone, or just for some people?

_____

_____

_____

_____

_____

_____

L. Are you more comfortable using prayers from books or periodicals, compared with spontaneous prayer, knowing that the words were crafted by an "expert"?

_____

_____

_____

_____

_____

_____

M. Who has responsibility for the vitality of ritual prayer: the leader, the participants, or all involved?

_____

_____

_____

_____

_____

_____

Prayer for the Dead

N. Do you feel that praying for the dead is helpful for the pray-er, helpful for the pray-ee, both, or neither? If neither, do you think it is harmful? If so, why?

_____

_____

_____

_____

_____

_____

O. What might one want to say to our Daddy when praying for the dead?

_____

_____

_____

_____

_____

_____

Praying Without Ceasing

P. Deep down inside, do you find the idea of praying without ceasing exciting, burdensome, frightening, impossible, or would you choose some other adjective?

If the latter, what adjective?

_____

_____

_____

_____

_____

_____

Q. How would you describe praying without ceasing in other words?

_____

_____

_____

_____

_____

_____

Christian Meditation

R. Are you comfortable with the idea of meditation as a Christian practice? Why or why not?

_____

_____

_____

_____

_____

_____

S. How would you describe the difference between prayer and meditation?

_____

_____

_____

_____

_____

_____

T. Do you consider prayer and meditation to be an "either-or" proposition? In other words, is one of them enough for a full Christian life, without the other?

_____

_____

_____

_____

_____

_____

U. Is Christian meditation different from Transcendental Meditation, and if so, how?

_____

_____

_____

_____

_____

_____

Praying in Jesus's Name

A. Do you always end a prayer with "in Jesus's name, amen"? If so, why? Do you feel that it makes your prayer more likely to be answered as you wish?

_____

_____

_____

_____

_____

_____

B. What does it mean to do something in someone else's name? Can you think of situations in everyday secular life when we do something in someone else's name? What about our business or professional lives? Our family lives? Acting under a power of attorney for a disabled person?

_____

_____

_____

_____

_____

_____

C. Find a Scripture passage in which we are instructed to pray in Jesus's name.

_____

_____

_____

_____

_____

_____

D. Do you think Jesus was giving us a magical formula for making prayer work when He gave us that instruction? If not, what do you think He meant: what was His purpose?

_____

_____

_____

_____

_____

_____

E. Comment on this question: "Is it of any use to pray in Jesus's name if we do not live our lives in His name?"

_____

_____

_____

Faith

A. Is faith the same as belief? Mental agreement or assent? How are the meanings of these words similar, and how are they different?

_____

_____

_____

_____

_____

_____

B. Can you give an example of faith in a non-Christian, non-religious context?

_____

_____

_____

_____

_____

_____

The Power of Faith

C. Are there limits to what faith can accomplish? If so, are these limitations built into the universe, or are they our own limitations?

_____

_____

_____

_____

_____

_____

D. Do you think the power of faith is at odds with modern science? If so, in which do you place more confidence?

_____

_____

_____

_____

_____

_____

E. Do you think there are sayings of Jesus quoted in Scripture that are not authentic, or that are no longer true? Was Jesus's knowledge "pre-scientific"?

_____

_____

_____

_____

_____

_____

Developing Faith

F. Name several areas in our secular lives in which we depend on faith, not on the evidence of our physical senses.

_____

_____

_____

_____

_____

_____

G. See if you can think of any activities in our daily lives in which we have no dependence on faith at all.

_____

_____

_____

_____

_____

_____

H. How does faith differ, depending upon whether it is considered in a secular or Christian context?

_____

_____

_____

_____

_____

_____

I. Do you wish for stronger faith? Why? How would you know if you had "stronger faith"? How would it impact your life?

_____

_____

_____

_____

J. How can we have stronger faith where spiritual matters are
    concerned?

_____

_____

_____

_____

_____

_____

Feeding Our Faith

K. What are two of your favorite Scripture passages that exemplify
    the power of faith? Summarize.

_____

_____

_____

_____

_____

_____

L. Describe two events that you have experienced or heard of that testify to the power of faith. These can be as simple as a mysterious sense of guidance that proved valuable.

_____

_____

_____

_____

_____

_____

M. How many tips could you offer for strengthening and using faith in your life? List as many as you can think of.

_____

_____

_____

_____

_____

_____

Preparation for Prayer

A. Are there any things you do to prepare yourself for prayer? These can be formal rituals or simple "attitude adjustments". List as many as you can.

_____

_____

_____

_____

_____

_____

B. Do you think all people are alike in how we should prepare for prayer, or do we differ significantly?

_____

_____

_____

_____

_____

_____

C. Do certain places, physical postures, spiritual disciplines, and/or companions incline you toward a good attitude for prayer? Give examples.

_____

_____

_____

_____

_____

_____

D. When we choose certain ways to prepare for prayer, is our purpose to attune ourselves, or to impress God?

_____

_____

_____

_____

_____

_____

E. Can our lifestyle itself be a preparation for prayer? Discuss.

_____

_____

_____

_____

_____

_____

Contemporary Holiness

A. There was a popular Gospel song in the 1950's called "Faith, Hope, and Charity". The first two lines of the chorus were:

> "Don't worry 'bout tomorrow,
> Just be real good today."

How well do these lines summarize Christian holiness?

_____

_____

_____

_____

_____

_____

B. If you were to name a person who embodies your ideal way to think, act, and live, who would that person be?

_____

_____

_____

_____

_____

_____

C. Name the most important spiritual, mental, and physical characteristics of that person.

_____

_____

_____

_____

_____

_____

D. In what ways do you really try to be like that person?

_____

_____

_____

_____

_____

_____

E. In what ways do you come close to succeeding?

_____

_____

_____

_____

_____

_____

F. In what ways do you fall short of your ideal?

_____

_____

_____

_____

_____

_____

G. Is it up to us to become more like our ideals, or is it up to God to make it happen? Is it perhaps a combination of both? Put another way, is it God's fault or our fault that we do not perfectly embody our ideals? Is more hard work on our part the key to improving?

_____

_____

_____

_____

_____

_____

H. Is it helpful for us to feel really guilty about falling short of our ideals?

_____

_____

_____

_____

_____

_____

I. If we fall short of our ideals, can we limit our improvement efforts to only spiritual, only mental, or only physical ones, or are they all somehow interconnected?

_____

_____

_____

_____

_____

_____

J. Personal performance coach Gary Craig has said that there are only two fundamental emotions: love and fear. If this is true, what sort of light does it shed for us on Jesus's commandment to love one another? To love our enemies? Do all methods of achieving holiness begin and end in love?

_____

_____

_____

_____

_____

_____

www.ingramcontent.com/pod-product-compliance
Lightning Source LLC
Chambersburg PA
CBHW060534030426
42337CB00021B/4262